I0203062

TIME MEASURED OUT!

Navigating Life's Journey Through Poetry

BOOK 2

LARADA HORNER-MILLER

HORNER PUBLISHING COMPANY

Copyright © 2025 by Larada Horner-Miller

To buy books in quantity for corporate use or incentives, call (505) 323-7098 or email larada@LaradasBooks.com

ISBN-13: 979-8-9896886-4-7 (Horner Publishing Company)

All rights reserved.

No part of this book may be reproduced in any form or by any electronic or mechanical means, including information storage and retrieval systems, without written permission from the author, except for the use of brief quotations in a book review.

🌸 Formatted with Vellum

PRAISE FOR LARADA HORNER-MILLER

A personal memoir read like prose but written in poetic form.

-Michael Sweet

❀

A very generous poet. I became absorbed in each facet of the life of which she writes. I tried setting parameters of reading time so I didn't consume the entire book immediately. I failed. In the end, I reread the book to better savor it the second time.

-Rhonda Long

❀

An unflinching and brilliant memoir of one woman's journey through heartbreak, resilience, and love. A must-read for poetry fans.

–Autumn Williams,
author of *Waves* and *Clouds on the Ground*

❀

Time Measured Out—Love this detail of the poem, not only of <u>time</u> but of <u>process</u> or <u>order</u>.

-Kathy Doherty,
Writer & Member of Colorado Writing Practice Writing Group

❀

Larada writes poems ripped from layers in her heart memories. Appealing to me as a person who struggles with depression are the lines when she questions her self worth in the poem of the *Washington Rain Forest*. "Eventually, I shine bright. In fact, I'm always shining bright! It's what's outside me that blocks the light Occasionally." Her poetry brings me hope.

-Sherrie L. Crandal
MEd

DEDICATION

- Always to my husband, Lin, for his astute curiosity about who I was as a writer and identified me being a poet
- Sherrie Crandal for her continued support of all of my books and her weekly response to my blog
- Poetry readers everywhere who have realized the power of poetry and its place in our world

"Poetry is an echo, asking a shadow to dance."

Carl Sandburg

CONTENTS

DISCOVER YOUR TRUTH IN VERSE

FREE Poetry Book

Is My Truth Universal?: A Woman's Poetic Odyssey

What happens when one woman's deeply personal journey becomes a mirror for us all? 🌑

Download your <u>FREE</u> copy today and discover how one woman's truth becomes everyone's journey. 🚗

Get yours **free**—because some truths are meant to be shared — at

https://laradasfreebook.com/truth

INTRODUCTION

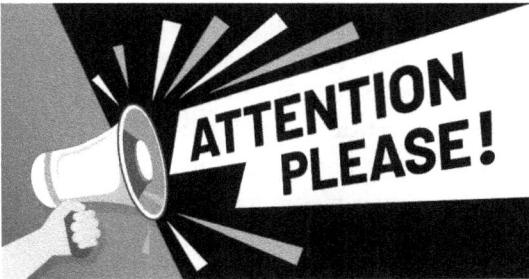

"Instructions for living a life:
Pay attention.
Be astonished.
Tell about it."

-Mary Oliver, "Sometimes"

Life's all about paying attention and not letting the world pass you by. Some call it mindfulness. That's a big order, but I see that's what I did over the years with my poetry by being present and seeing the specifics in my life around me. Prior to writing poetry and taking note of my life, years escaped me! The poet arose in me, and this is what transpires: I write poetry when I'm happy, when I'm sad. I write about what's important—and about what's trivial.

And now you're getting a peek into me. Not only am I sharing the vulnerability in my poetry, but in my life.

This is the second book of poetry in a five-book poetry series that chronicles my journey from 1986 to the present, showcasing both difficult times and, ultimately, my most fulfilling era. It all changed at fifty-eight and my fourth marriage, but that's much later, in book #5.

My first book in this series, *Was It a Dream?: Navigating Life's Journey Through Poetry*, which covered my life in poetry from 1986 to 1998, won a Gold Award in the Global Book Awards and second place for poetry in the Next Best Reads Writing Contest, which felt so affirming.

When I choose a title for my books, I consult my husband. I gave him the list of poems chronicling my life from 2000-2003, and he quickly came up with *Time Measured Out*. I love how this title captures not only the transformative time this was for me, but my playfulness in poetry, as well.

So much happened in the years this book covers, not just for me personally, but also globally. Because I worked as a middle school teacher, I did a lot of my writing during the summer, sitting in the passenger seat, my ex-husband driving down the road to the next square and round dance festival. The summers were my time to write, to travel, to get away from the crushing schedule of teaching, and to see our country near and far—and to dance!

In 2000, my ex-husband, Ted, and I bought a Four Winds Majestic Flyer Class C motorhome in preparation for our 2001 road trip to Alaska on the Al-Can Highway. I dubbed the summer of 2000 "The Majestic Flyer Summer," after our RV, as we tested it out while traveling to dance festivals.

We spent hours planning our Alaska trip, and my excitement grew as we prepared. We traveled north to the Canadian border then followed the Al-Can Highway from Dawson Creek, British Columbia, to Delta Junction, Alaska, via Whitehorse, Yukon. The rough uneven roads made it an adventure for me, but Ted as the driver grew tired of it. But our journey didn't go how either of us expected. We broke up in Homer, Alaska in one of the most picturesque spots, the ocean surrounding us. Ted took me to Anchorage to my cousin, then I flew home, leaving him to drive the RV back.

After our breakup, I sought refuge at the Santuario de Chimayó for the second time, but how different my experience was this time compared to my first visit in 1991 (see book #1)!

My ex-husband and I tried to resolve our differences for seven more years, but our reconciliation didn't fare smoothly. We did have some good times sprinkled in, but it was mostly trouble, chaos, and agony. We struggled until 2008, and I share our final breakup in book #4. Amid this, I continued to turn to poetry to make sense of life—my writing comforted me and helped me survive, and survive I did!

Though there've been deep struggles in my life, my positivity always weaves its way through. In this book, you'll see me repeatedly struggle with my relationship with my ex-husband and how I viewed myself because of it—a dysfunctional relationship at its worst! Yet I bounced back, resilient. If you've had similar experiences, resilience saved our lives!

The book will draw near its end with poems I wrote in celebration of my niece for her thirtieth birthday and, lastly, a tribute to my mom. Ending this book with my thoughts about Mom brings a smile to my lips and an ache to my heart! Yes, Mom, you end this second book—so apropos!

Just a reminder! Someone wrote this comment in a review on Goodreads about *Was It a Dream?*: "There were a few places where these poems felt amateur. In some ways that adds to the charm, but I can't help wanting to poke at them and try to use one of the many tools we have to make poetry more effective."

Please remember this poetry series dates back to 1986, and I didn't polish any of the poems. I wanted you, the reader, to see my progression through the years as a poet. Refraining from "fixing" them felt risky, yet I committed myself and you to this journey. And, yes—it's been hard!

Step into my world of poetry, and don't look back. You might decide to grab a seat and linger or even stay.

Chapter One

2000

Let's start this book with romance—love for a man and love for the road and the journey.

A SPECIAL MOMENT

May 12, 2000

How can one moment be so special,
  One isolated space in time
    That is seared in my memory
      Forever.

The square dance tip ended—
  I had danced with another.
I looked for you
  People blocked our view.
  Heads, shoulders,
  A sea of smiling faces.

Then I saw you—
  Our eyes caught,
  And it happened.

A tug at my heart,
 And earthquake in my soul,
 A deep knowing of my spirit.

All others faded away
 To a soft melodic background.
All I saw was you,
 The joy in your eyes!
The deep knowing as I joined you!

Ted, I could never have loved you
 More than I did at that moment!

IT'S A ROMANCE!

May 12, 2000

It's a romance
 An obsession
  A tug that pulls at
   my heartstrings.

The view before us—
 a white lane racing
  Toward the next place,
   The next stop.

Mountains, deserts, beaches, plains!
 It's a romance with—
  The road
   The journey
    The going
     The new
      The adventure!

5

Where does it lead?
    Does it matter?
Where are we going?
    Who cares?

It's a romance!
      A lover—
    Seductive and sensual
    Luscious and warm
    Satisfying deeper than life itself.

The seat beside you,
    Heading down the road
To our next dance,
    Campsite,
    National park,
    Whatever!

It's a romance
    With the journey!

Chapter Two

2000 – SKETCHBOOK

In 2000, I bought an oversized sketchbook and used it as my writing journal during the summer as my ex-husband and I traveled the country in our brand-new Majestic Flyer RV. We bought it to drive the Al-Can Highway to Alaska in 2001. Beforehand, we wanted to practice with our new home and get the kinks out.

Because I was a teacher, we could travel the USA in the summer, and this RV became our home. Our destination— square and round dance festivals across the country. And my joy of the world around us as we traveled was captured in poetry.

In this notebook, I focused on our relationship and the landscape surrounding us in our beautiful country, especially along the western coast from California to Washington. While I wrote, Ted drove us down the road.

I end this chapter with musings about our home and a heartbreaking episode in my dance world.

In this sketchbook, I jotted down phrases I heard along the way and thoughts I had and observations:

- June 1, 2000 – "Did you stop to think and forget to get started again?" Salt Lake City, Utah
- June 2, 2000 – "I'm drawn to paint horses"
- June 7, 2000 – By Randolph, Utah, all over the meadows the hay is piled then a fence around them. They used a beaver slide to harvest, not bales. I had never seen a beaver slide before!
- June 8, 2000 – Going in to Vernal, Utah, there are ten switchbacks and signs warning you, "Nine more" and "Five more" and so on
- June 8, 2000 – An old drive-in theater in Craig, Colorado. Drive-in theaters had been a wonderful part of my early life in Trinidad, Colorado!

As I look back at these thoughts, I laugh out loud because I've always been a word and language person. Capturing these phrases and observations is just something I do!

THE SEASCAPE

July 11, 2000
Northern California

The Seascape—the northern shores of
  California
  Pounding, crashing waves
  No longer sandy beaches to walk on.
    Rocks
  An escape of sound as the waves
  recede.

The sea
  A violent creature
  Tearing up Mother Earth
  Grabbing ahold of and selfishly
    letting go all that it can.

Fog rolls in
    Covers everything
    Misty, damp, melancholy.

In San Francisco,
    Foghorns sound all night.
        Eerie—repetitive
        A bull echoing its desires.

The ocean speaks deeply to me.
    The rhythm and cadence,
        My own.
    I ebb and flow.
    I am moist, teeming with life.
    Violent emotions rage in my heart
    That want to explode!

The sadness of life overwhelms me
    A breaking heart
    A need for love
        More frustrating than no love at all.

WHY WOULD SHE?

July 17, 2000
Washington Rain Forest

"Why would she want to be with you?
    Why would she want to talk to you?"

Two searing questions stated!

Why would anyone want to be with me,
    talk to me?
A question I have hidden very deep in my
    heart.

The quiet green trees
Sunlight flickers through the branches as
    we pass.
    An abundance of water
        The Pacific Ocean,
            Lakes, streams, creeks!

Reflections of my inner self.
I am a quiet, green tree, deeply rooted
    Rich, green color sprouting,
        health, and vigor.

I am sunlight—
    The power to shine
    The power to warm and heal.

I flicker through the growth
    around me—
    but,
    Eventually, I shine bright.
In fact, I'm always shining bright!
It's what's outside me
    that blocks the light
        Occasionally.

I am water
    Fluid, flowing
    Life-giving
    Full, Rich, Comforting

That's why!

ANTICIPATE THE JOY!

July 24, 2000

Anticipate the joy
   Toes on the edge
   Lingering ever so slightly,
     But ready to plunge!

Life in its fullness
   Step out on the dance floor
   Step up to bat
   Step into the swimming pool,
     No, dive head long!
   Step out of the crowd
   Step into the crowd

I must participate
   I can't watch
   Wasn't made to watch,
   To be the spectator.

I want my hands dirty
   My neck sweaty
   My feet wet
I want to experience life totally.

☙

Green canopy
   Variegated colors
     Yet all green.
Sunlight filters through,
   Dancing like a spider.
The damp air trapped beneath
   The green—wet and moist.
A silence loud and clear.
No rush, no hurry
Just time to be.

☙

Crashing waves
Rhythm of Earth
Magic of movement
Frothy violence
Life flows
   In and out
Crashes, pounds
Bliss and horror
   All at once.
Juxtaposition of life.

☙

A wealth of water
   The sea
      Lakes
      Streams
      Creeks
Green, lush, verdant
The cycle's end
An open horizon
Life goes on forever.

The deep northwest forest
   Closed in
   Captured
   No space.

🦋

My spacious place has enlarged
   Grown
   Expanded!

It encompasses much more
   The mountains
   The ocean
   The mesa
The west
The north
Canada
The Pacific coast
The northwest
Trees
Beaches
Surfers

Cool cliffs that overhang the beaches
Pelicans
Sea lions
Seagulls
Whales

As it grows, I grow.
I see me more clearly!
The motive is the core
    The attitude.

THERE IS A HOUSE!

September 17, 2000

There is a house at 515 Eugene Court SE,
    Albuquerque, New Mexico,
        That came to be because
           of a Question—
Would you like to live together?
    —and a dream.

It was a vacant space
    overlooking an arroyo—
Only a couple other houses built nearby.

This site; that one!
    The decision was hard!
The one we wanted got away,
    but God knew better
        and saved the best for us.

The process was magic:
a foundation
   with pipes sticking up like antlers
a puzzle
   the walls
then the roof
   the vigas
      stately support logs
         To decorate the ceiling.

The process—
   watching you enjoy,
   pinching me to see if it was real.

Friends moved me in
   my stuff made this house mine—ours.
      It felt shared!

We caravanned your belongings
   from Idaho.
You asked me questions,
   opinions along the way.
I urged you to place the window
   in the great room
   a question because of the deck.
      The decision, a good one.
Three years of mixing yours and mine
   has made it ours!

A home,
   a place to hang your hat
      your coat,
a place some famous person said
   they have to let you in.

A home
   grown larger than the boards
      and nails that hold it together.
   A safe place
     we've lived here, loved here,
        fought here, cried here, but
        mostly listened here
           deeply to each other!

Yes, Ted, you do have a home!
515 Eugene Court SE
   stucco and mortar
   stable
   comfortable
   gorgeous!

I know you said you bought this
   only as an investment,
but I think the dividends
   have exceeded your plans.
You thought you made a wise investment
   into a house and real estate
     and what you got was a home!
Priceless!!

SPIRIT COYOTE

September 20, 2000
A Walk Near Our House

One soft quiet dawn I see you
and my deep heart knows.
We know each other profoundly
beyond time and space.

Your eyes haunt me
following my every move.
Your home,
a sacred Indian burial ground,
separated from the world and me
by a chain-link fence.
Ancient ones honored!

I walk by here daily on the outside—
you and them gather together today
on the inside.

Are you coyote? Are you spirit?
   I can't be sure!
I question as I'm mesmerized by you.
    You turn away from me,
        and I recognize your lean frame.
You are coyote!

Death has captured them
   and you, too,
      or are you captured?
Are you dead?
  Are you free?

You follow my moves;
   stealthily you step toward me.
I gulp worried you will charge,
   but your movement toward me stops.
Now you move with me, alongside me.

I feel comfort in your presence—
   no fear,
      a companion that knows my heart.
You rise up on a small mound
   then you're gone—gone forever!

A chain-link fence separates us.
   You locked in with the dead,
      me alive outside,
        walking free,
          yet skirting you and death.
            Are you here every day?

TIME MEASURED OUT!

At times, I hear the chains in the fence
    rattle in the breeze,
        yet I know it's not the breeze—
            the sound is too severe.
        I know it's spirits,
            like you caught in that place,
                that place between
                    the unknown,
                        a place I know so well!

We are one; I see it!
Death, spirit coyote, and me
    roaming through this life!
Those ancient ones inside me clamor
    to be free, to be put to rest!

Your spirit sought me out
    with a message.
Some natives see you as the trickster,
    the predator by ranchers.
Others see you as the tourist symbol
    of the Southwest
        and place a red bandana
            around your neck.
                What a shame!

Your spirit is larger, filling the arroyo
   and canyon of my heart.
You roam free—
   so, take me along!
I yearn to roam free,
   to howl at the moon,
           at my loneliness,
           at my aloneness,
           at the other spirits
              walking my same path.

HOW IS A HOME MADE?

October 15, 2000

Homemaker
happy homemaker
how is a home made?

Splashes of me on the walls,
snippets of me on the coffee table.
A refrigerator covered with my magnets:
    favorite quotes
        words that burn a new memory
            deep inside me
                Pictures
                Memorabilia
Yes, a home is made!

Stiff lumber, straight wall lines,
    a slanted roof
        construct a house,
        but I want a home,
        and I get to make it.

I create it,
    with the warmth of me.
My things,
    the clutter that's familiar.
It's me!

It's been in a variety of packages:
    a small 1 bedroom apartment
        in Denver
    a larger 2 bedroom apartment
        in Denver
    a small 2 bedroom house
        in Denver
    a larger 3 bedroom ranch style
        in Loveland
    a long, skinny 3 bedroom mobile home
        in Loveland
            Fort Collins
                North Glen
                Raton
    a small studio apartment
        in Albuquerque
    an old 2 bedroom fixer-upper
        in the North Valley of Albuquerque
Now,
    a spacious beautiful 3 bedroom stucco
        palace in Albuquerque.

But it's also been in
    a tent
    my camper
    our RV
    an airplane
    Mayan Indian ruins in Coba
    an Anasazi ruin in Chaco Canyon.

And it has also been
    in the forest amongst the trees
    with Dad in Branson
       and on the ranch
    in the sweat lodge
       and the spiritual heart of
          the Native people
    in a good book
    in my writing
    on the beach at Playa Del Carmen

It's large because it's the world—
    my spacious place I've created!

WHAT I KNOW!

October 15, 2000

What I know is the spirit life.
  Today it is sad
    Running over with grief and loss.
  I fight it,
    Punching thin air,
    There's no one there—
  No one but my loss!

It may change to serenity and peace,
  Adding a charge of sunshine
    to the darkest day.
I accept it,
  Caressing it close to my heart
  Softly touching the wings extended
Knowing its possibility of flight.

It may be chaos—
   Something I know deeply
      The churning excessive activity
       The nameless, anxiety,
        belching fumes of
         Bitter herbs.
     The impending doom,
      The loss that will be
       But isn't
        But I anticipate
       But isn't
        But I know will happen
       Because it has so often
         in the past
       But hasn't yet.
       The fear that
         it's all in vain,
          There's no point
         Why go on?

This is all the spiritual life
  The ebb and flow,
  Because my God meets me in the sad
    With tears
      In the serenity and peace
    With open arms and a smile
      In the chaos
    With His knowing
    With the shoulder to lean
    With His presence and guidance.

REALITY TAKES DIFFERENT FACES

We had just danced the weekend away in Montgomery, Alabama. Ted drove, and I flew; that was our routine because I was still teaching. He flirted the weekend away with other women. Sitting in the airport in Houston, the woman he flirted with most sat down beside me, trying to make small talk. This poem helped me survive!

> December 3, 2000
> Houston Lobby Airport
> After Montgomery, Alabama weekend

Reality takes different faces—
A punctured weekend
  Bleeding and wounded
A special time gone sour
Because truth raised its ugly head!

I see you and you're an illusion!
The image I've conjured in my head.

It's not your fault you don't match it—
　　It's mine!

More was shattered this weekend
　　Which will allow me to release
　　　　More
　　　　Face more
　　　　Let go more!
I can't hold on forever!
　　I can't love in the old way!
　　I can't assume!
　　I can't control!
　　I can't be that person I was yesterday,
　　　　this morning.

　　My spirit demands more.
　　My spirit demands authenticity,
　　　　Gentleness
　　　　　　Peace
　　　　　　　　Happiness.

I am a mix though,
　　And I know it!
I have no regrets about this weekend.
I faced the enemy and won.
I am not crazy, no matter what Ted says!
I know deeply my truth.
　　I'm a mysterious mix of manure
　　　　and star dust!
　　　　　　Of angel's wings and pain!
I'm not either or,
　　and I'm not bad, wrong, or stupid!

Chapter Three

2001 – SKETCHBOOK CONTINUES

The summer of 2001, my ex-husband and I drove to Alaska on the Al-Can highway, and I grabbed my trusty sketchbook to record the trip.

I enjoyed the trip up to Denali National Park in the green school bus. I didn't see Mt. McKinley when we were in the park, but later that day I did!

And of course, my poetry matched the scenery but during that trip, I wrote only two poems about God's gorgeous world.

Instead, I addressed the emotional pain I continued to grapple with along the way, as well as what appeared to be the end of our relationship—though it didn't end quite yet.

When I returned home, in my sadness, I returned to the Santuario de Chimayó and struggled with the priest's response to me about denying me communion.

Santuario de Chimayó - Taken by Larada Horner-Miller

And then September 11th happened. I include my heart-broken appraisal of that fateful day in 2001. I stood in my bedroom, dressing for work that day, watching the news in horror as the first tower came down.

When I got to school, my middle school students sat glued to the TV in my classroom in each class. Many students had parents who worked on Kirtland Air Force base. I heard rumors about helicopters circling the base in case of attack. I tried to console my students each period, but we had just crossed over into uncharted territory.

THE SILENCE SPEAKS LOUDLY!

June 8, 2001
Pocahontas Campground
Jasper National Park

The silence speaks loudly!
   The quiet
   The sound of trees makes it so loud.
      The grass

The peace
   The calm I yearn for.

The fire crackles,
   Devouring its wood
   And changing its form.
The process,
   One similar to mine.

It's the quiet, the simple slowness,
   the deliberate pace
      I seek.

Lightyears from the rush of my life!
I've stopped.
   I've quieted.
      I've deliberately paused.

The fire warms my feet and soul.
The smoke transports me to happy times
   Around the campfire.

A group of misfits committed to a
   summer of fun.
   A summer like no other
   —Shared readings
   —Shared lives
   —Shared laughter and pain

I look for that same kind of bond every
   summer now,
   But it's gone!

LIFE TAKES TIME!

June 8, 2001
Pocahontas Campground
Jasper National Park

Life takes time!
    To see the wonder
    To hear the joy
    To smell the fragrance.

I've tried for years to rush it.
    Today, I understand—
        It takes time.
Time to be comfortable with me,
    With all the oddities,
    With all the surprises.

I wanted it yesterday.
    I couldn't wait for tomorrow.
I didn't realize it was only in today!

THE SPIRIT OF DENALI

Land that went on forever
    The vastness
    The beauty
Wildlife—not abundant, but there.
The spirit of the place filled me.

A cool damp day
    Riding a green school bus,
Forty-six other passengers.
Anticipation held me tight all day!

My first time seeing grizzly bears
    In the wild!
        Blonde dots on the hillside.
Dall sheep
    White dots.

A caribou in full glory raced the edge
    Of the hill above me.
I fumbled
    Excited
    Caught off guard
    New camera
    No pictures.

Only a memory—
    Surreal—a caribou dancing
        On my head!

Dall Ram - Taken by Larada Horner-Miller

A dall ram situated on a cliff
    Regal
    Pensive
    Posing for me.

We arrived at Eiselson Visitor Center—
    No time for lunch
    Time for exploring.

Mt. McKinley - Denali - Taken by Larada Horner-Miller

Mount McKinley
 Hidden
 Shrouded in clouds
 Twenty percent get to see it, not me
  That day, but another.
 A mystery
The view I see surrounds me
 360 degrees of mountains
  Envelops me
  With grandeur
What my spacious place would be

God in His glory.
 I watched, waited,
  Drank in every ounce of it I could.
I didn't want it to end—eight hours,
 Not enough.

My spirit is thirsty.
 It needs more.

The beauty satisfies a thirst so deep in
    my soul.
God made it—the beauty of Alaska
God made me—the beauty of Larada
    Out of the same soil
Our roots go deep,
    Deep into the heart of God.

A VACATION

July 27, 2001

I want a vacation from me
  From the pain.

THE POWER OF PAIN

July 30, 2001

The power of the pain
    Forces me to look deeply.
What happened to me?
    Why did I quit?
I had nothing more to give.
    Drained totally.

The exchange was short,
    Two minutes at max,
And it ended our vacation
    And our relationship.
What happened?
    Reactions totally!
    Two hurt little kids
        Shutting down totally!

No argument
  Yelling
  Demands
  Suggestions
  Cut off from communication.

A beautiful backdrop of this world,
  Alaska—
    Totally darkened.

I could do nothing!
  Frozen
  Shut down
  No hugs to offer
  Nothing
I could do nothing!

Then he said it was over,
And I ran
  To organize
  To set up
  To gather support.

And I ran
  Away
  Totally
  Alone.

I've never physically
    Ran before.
I've left emotionally,
    But this time I ran.
My heart cracked in two.
    The split echoed
        In my ears.

He said my asking to leave
    One day early ruined
        His vacation—
So I did, I left!

But I didn't think it
    Would!
I thought he'd go on—
    I didn't perceive
        him clearly.
I really thought it
    Was over this time.

I LOOKED FOR A RETREAT

August 1, 2001
Santuario de Chimayó

I looked for a retreat
  A pilgrimage,
So I did what a lot of
  New Mexicans do—
    I drove to Santuario de Chimayó.
My spirit needed some dirt,
  Some holy dirt.

I promised my friend Lorraine some
  For her chemotherapy
  For her spirit.
I promised NanDie some
  For her heart
  For her spirit.
I promised Yolanda some

For her alcoholism
For her spirit.

I rose early and
   Arrived on time.
Directly I went to the sacred hole and
   Filled two bags.
I cried—I felt relief.

I noticed mass at 11 o'clock—
   How lucky!

I shopped, then I "massed,"
   And that's when reality hit.

I enthusiastically rose to join
   The line
      For communion.
The priest said, "The body of Christ."
I said, "The bread of heaven."
He repeated his phrase.
I repeated mine.
"Are you Catholic?"
"I'm Episcopalian."
"You can't have communion.
   You were supposed to say "Amen.""

I knew that!
I've done this thousands of times—
   Said, "Amen!" for the bread and the
   wine—
But refused communion, **never**!

That priest didn't see my broken heart,
    My tears,
    My pain.
He refused me his solution to my stress,
    But Jesus would not have—
    Buddha would not have!

What have these traditional religious
    Organizations come to?
    A password—
    The right faith!
Did Jesus ask for the right faith?
Did he refuse anyone?
    I don't think so.

Can I refuse anyone healing?
Can I say I'm better than you,
    Don't hurt?
No—I don't think so.

Can I refuse Ted the opportunity to heal?
    Can I refuse me that same
     opportunity?
No!

My world is larger than that.

My God is more open than that.
    He lets me come to him,
       However I can,
          Ragged, snotty nose, drooling.
He accepts my pain in whatever form
    It is in.

Refused communion
    On this day of pilgrimage!
But not refused God
    No one has that power—no priest!
        No man!

I'm seeking a more gentle, loving,
    Compassionate way.
    One that is full of God, love,
        and spaciousness.

My spacious place is large,
    Including all,
    Refusing none.
It's the mesa line,
    Open and stark.
It's the mountain glacier,
    Sparkling white in the bright sunlight.
It's the ocean, the sea,
    The wetness of new life.
It's everywhere and everyone.
I can connect to wherever I am,
    Because it grows from inside of me.

❦

People come and go at a regular pace
    To visit this holy New Mexico sight.
They look;
    They're awed!
But what brings them here?
    Rumor

Advertisement
Spirit
It's calm
No loud voices
No loud spirits

A puppy, too!

It's peaceful
A step back in time
A sleepy Hispanic village
Focused on the church,
The spirit of the community.

Seventy miles away
Albuquerque bustles to a different
tune.
Horns honk, the pulse beats,
Activity frantic to keep up
Or rush ahead.

Chimayó
Relaxes in the shade
Of cottonwood trees
Sells its wares of tourism
But there's reverence here
It's more than a tourist trap!

Hundreds to thousands have sought
Healing here
And found it.
Somehow, the dirt, the earth

God's basic material turned
   Miraculous.
So people come, curious
          Expectant
          Suspicious,
But they come!

What did I come for?
   A respite
   An answer
     Peace, and I found all three.

I found it in the place,
   Not in the ceremony
   Not in the priest.
I found it in the church
   In the dirt
In the solidity of God's love
   And acceptance.
I found it in my heart
   because it was already there.

I really received nothing here
   I couldn't have found at home.

Because what I found was me—
   The deeply loving,
      Compassionate woman that I am.
I found universal love
   Big love
   Accepting love
      Deep in my heart for me.

No priest can ruin this day for me,
　　Unless I let him.
He taught me a lesson—
　　How big is your love, Larada?

WATCHING PEOPLE IN CHIMAYÓ

August 1, 2001
Santuario de Chimayó

He snaps a picture.
    She does.
He surveys the right space
    Fiddles with equipment
    Takes one here
    Takes one there
    Takes one down on his knees.

Picture taking—
    Capture the moment,
        The place,
    But can it be, really?

Art?
    Aesthetics?

Driven by a need,
   A need to hold on
      To capture something
      To hold it in space and time.

It's control!
It's a need!
I need to save this
   Because I may not get another.

Crippled people come—
For healing
Deep belief that God lives here
   And works here.

A woman sits on the ledge by the creek
   Her partner takes pictures.
Shades cover her eyes,
   But he knows she weeps.
He comforts her.
Where do her tears come from?
What brings her brokenness here?
She retreats to the restroom
   And refreshes.
He greets her return
   With a hug and
      A kiss on her head, on her hair.
They now enter the santuario
   For the first time.
Twenty minutes it took for her to
   be able
   To go inside.
Deep pain separates her from her God.

❀

Two artists set up their wares.
    Ready to paint this monument.
Two older women,
    The New Mexican kind
        One has long gray hair and a
    ponytail
            And a ball cap,
        Big sloppy T-shirt and skirt.
            Artist!

❀

My day has been successful.
    I've retreated.
    I've stopped the cycle.
    I've taken a step back in time
        To quiet and reclusion.

❀

Humanity has passed me
        these few hours.
    I am here alone,
        Yet a part of.
    I am a seeker,
        A warrior on the path.
    I want spirit and soul
        More than anything.
    I want God
    I want Larada,
    And in the midst of this,

I will find peace.

The thunder rolls in the distance.
    God speaks.
The gentle breeze blows.
    God speaks.
I sob my tears.
    God speaks.
The priest refused me communion.
    God speaks.

It's all been a day of collection,
    Collecting all I need today
        For my journey.

A maturity covers me.
    The thunder grows louder.
Last time I was here it snowed.
    The season changes.
    Life changes.
    I change.

I can have it all!
    All that I want!

I TRIED AND TRIED

August 4, 2001
After Walking

I tried and tried my whole life,
   And I'm tired!
      Bone tired
      Forty-eight years tired!

I've tried to fit in,
   To understand
   To make sense of the senselessness
      In my life.
Today I resigned.

I asked my God to wrap me
   In a shroud of Mother Earth
      For protection,
Completely cover me with the warmth
   Of this earth.

I see the mesa line mysterious
    Across my shoulders
  The plains across my breast
    Flat and rolling
  The Alaska range across my hips.
    Glacial turquoise water
      Streams and lakes
        Undulate cross me and
    Protect me from the invasion.
The ocean around my feet
  Wet and cool
  Safe and loving

I need protection;
I need help;
I need solace.
  Give it to me today, dear God.
Remind me of this comforting shroud.
Let it be full of animals and creatures.

Let my heart rejoice in your creation.
You cover me with dirt,
  The magical ingredient of life
Let me feel the warmth as it
  Lays heavy across me!
Bury me in the love that is.

MY FAVORITE THING TO TAKE PICTURES OF

August 4, 2001
After Walking

My favorite thing to take pictures of
    Is not the beautiful scenery we saw
        The wildlife that spoke so
            Deeply to my heart.

No.
It was you, Ted!

It captured a part of my heart
    To zoom in on you
    To set you up with the beauty
        Surrounding you!
    To see your eyes twinkle
    To catch you unaware
        And capture that moment.

Yes, by far
   You're my favorite subject
      To look through my lens
      And say "Smile."
      To love you deeply
         And hold that moment forever
In the little picture.

TODAY I SAT

August 4, 2001
After Walking

Today, at a recovery meeting,
   I sat beside Joe
      Laughter
      Gentle hugs and touches
         Throughout
A total victory and healing for me.

I hated Joe six, seven years ago.
We went nose-to-nose at a
   Group Conscious meeting
My side was right;
   His was wrong!
I couldn't stand being in the
   Same room as him.

Six months to a year later,
He went out
　　Started drinking again
And I started praying—
　　That special prayer
　　　　Every day,
"God, give Joe all the good things
　　I want."

He came back,
　　And I wept—
　　　　Tears of joy that he was back.
And he went out
And came back
　　And went out.

Now, he's back!
　　More than thirty days.
Today he sat beside me
　　At a meeting
　　Shoulder-to-shoulder—friends
And I knew deeply
　　That I was healed!
And that my God is big!

THE CANYON OF MY HEART

August 6, 2021

The canyon of my heart
Has turned into a glacier!

MY WORLD WAS SAFE OR WAS IT?

September 13, 2001

My world was safe—
    It was safe enough
        To trust to have a package left
            At my door—
        No more!
    It was safe enough
        To leave for work in the morning
            and know that I'd come home
                That night—
        No more!
    It was safe enough
        To travel in an airplane anywhere
            In the USA without fear—
        No more!
    It was safe enough
        To believe my neighbor

Could be trusted
    Even if his skin color differed
    From mine—
No more!

Chapter Four

2002 - SKETCHBOOK

My writing in my sketchbook continues in 2002, and I face another bad experience and another possible breakup with Ted after our trip to Myrtle Beach, South Carolina for a New Year's Eve round dance festival. This was our second time there for this festival. Our first was in 1997, and what a great time we had!

This time our relationship faltered once again, as it did so often.

I CHOKE BACK THE TEARS

January 9, 2002

I choke back the tears
    As I face my life.
Illusions smashed to nothingness!
Pain so real I can taste it.
What are the images?

The insanity stops with me.
    No child will carry it on!
    No product of me will go on.
    No more Laradas.

It's over.
The illusion smashed on the beaches
    Of Myrtle Beach
        By a book!

I feel so alone
    So raw
    Busted open.

What have my motives been?
    To whom do I owe an amend?
    What was my part?

More than anything
    To run away
    To hide
    To ease the pain the best I could.

Today I choke on the pain
    It gags me
    It grips me by the throat
        And says, "Die!"

But I don't want to die!
I want Sue to love me.
I want Larraine to love me.
I want Ted to love me!
But I'm powerless!
I have to let go and let God!

I ETCH MY LIFE

January 17, 2002

I etch my life with me.
    Small pieces drawn on the edge,
        The margin.
In the center, me:
    A robust, powerful woman;
And me:
    A fragile girl child.
I work hard at a collaboration
    A blend
    A mixture
My laugh, I love!
    A joyful bell tingling in my heart
        And soul.

NOW, I'M THAT GENERATION

April 17, 2002
After Poetry Alliance

I'm that generation now,
    The Oldies Station

I hear "Crystal Blue Persuasion"
    And am transported back
    Thirty years or more!

Could it be—thirty years?

An innocent teenager's heart
    Touched by this song,
    Then and now.

I wandered down life's path,
    Lost for so many years,
    Then recently re-found.

And the song has the same power.
　　My heart softens
　　　　I crawl inside and wish
　　　　　　For all that wasn't!
I used to wish for all that could be!

A song evokes that for me,
　　Transportation back to that moment.

THE AGONY LIVES ON IN ME!

April 17, 2002
After Poetry Alliance

The pole kept him erect.
  Dazed, he was drunk,
    Propped up!
  Supported by the nothingness
    That booze creates.
The sadness,
  The pain
Crosses my memory
  As I connect to the drunk in me.

It stole my life
  Left me for dead
    An empty vessel
      That craved to be full
      Of alcohol
      Of penises

Of food!

But nothing filled it,
    So the devastation went out!
Beating me to death,
    Sip by sip!

The agony lives on in me.
    When I see a man propped
        Up by a lamp pole—
    His despair so vast
        I fall in it
            For just a moment.

A good reminder.

DREAMS

April 17, 2002
After Poetry Alliance

The images crush together in a
    Small room in my mind—
    Too numerous to count.
They visit me regularly.
    Some I like;
        Some I don't.
George Strait looked me in the eye
    And said, "Make life happen!"[1]

---

1. See George Strait's advice in my poem in *Was it A Dream?: Navigating Life's Journey Through Poetry*, book #1, on page 79.

TIME MEASURED OUT

July 22, 2002
Thatcher, Idaho

Nine drops of Miracle-Gro
  To one quart of water,
    My house plants' weekly diet.
Eight minutes to bake one potato
  In the microwave.

Time measured out in bits and pieces.
  Lives divided so.

It's all a cycle,
  the seasons,
    the days,
      the years!

Where is it all going
  in such an orderly manner?

TIME

July 25, 2002
Provo River Campground, Utah

The time piece clicks on
   One second at a time.
My life dictates
   That I answer to that clock.

Does God have a clock?
   Are His minutes as short as mine?

IF YOU NEVER

July 25, 2002
Provo River Campground, Utah

If you never ask how I am,
    You never have to know the answer.
If you never speak first,
    Yours are always answers,
        never questions.
If you sit in silence waiting,
    My silence bangs up noisily
    against yours,
        And it's gone.
If you build your wall too high, I stop
    trying to break over it.
We have nothing!

My illusion shattered again
    For the umpteenth time.
You will never be

a caring, compassionate partner
    Because you can't.
I will always have that expectation
   With the motive of you caring for me,
   But you can't.
That expectation needs to be shattered.

The river rolls on freely—
   Bumping gently against rocks
     in the way.
It has a purpose
   A goal
As does all nature!

I roll freely—
   Bumping roughly against the rocks
     in my way.
I lose my purpose easily
   And am distracted!

I can't hear you, God!
   The clamor in my heart and head are
     too loud.
I can't feel you, God!
   The clamor drowns you out.
I can't smell you, God!
   The clamor cuts me off.
I can't taste you, God!
   The clamor drowns me out.
I can't see you, God!
   The clamor cuts me off.

It's the clamor I need rid of!

I DWELL IN POSSIBILITY!

I fashioned this poem after Emily Dickinson's "I Dwell in Possibility."

July 26, 2002

I dwell in possibility . . .

It's a rich life
    full to the brim.
I face it in every question
    that comes.
I move from abundance.
I have all I need.
I have all I want.
    What a sweet refuge!

Life can come and go,
    but my worry is set at ease
        because of my attitude.

No one can crash through my armor,
    because I am safe and warm.

It's a life of plenty,
    of abundance.
I have no worries left.

My God supplies it all!

OUR NAMES

I am named after both of my grandmothers, and this poem tells the story of my name, "Larada," my paternal grandmother. I grew up in the same town as she, and she had a major influence on me and my femininity.

August 1, 2002

We share our names,
   Not surnames,
   But given names.

I was named after you,
   You after your grandmother.
You never went by our name.
   I have my whole life.

When I introduce myself
   To people,
I introduce you.

So you've remained with me
    After your death
    After my tears fell often
      From your sharp tongue
    After I walked away
      With nothing,
But your name!

Does your sharp tongue escape
    Occasionally
    And speak through me?
Are you the spirit I contend with?
Do those harsh words reside
    in our names?

EVERY NIGHT AS A CHILD

Dad died January 6, 1996, and my loss continued.

August 24, 2002

Every night as a child,
   when you tucked me into bed,
      I clasped your neck,
     not wanting you to leave,
        desperate, frantic.

The lump that's in my throat tonight
   has sat there deep in my throat,
   for nearly 50 years—
   blocking my air, my thoughts, my life!
     I didn't want you to go!

I knew back then
   you would leave.
Your slipping through my bedroom door

after I fell asleep
safe in your embrace
would eventually be you slipping
out of my life,
Gone—forever.
I didn't want you to go!

I knew back then
I'd be left.
The door slammed shut—
a hollow echo in my childish dreams—
with me inside, and you gone!

I knew back then
I'd lose you.
That I'd grow up;
you'd grow old.
Then you'd be gone.
I didn't want you to go.

But wanting didn't stop it!
I lost you six years ago.
Death and cigarettes took you away
too early
too quickly!

I wanted to share today
with you,
the laughter with Mom
my place I've created
Dance-A-Rama 2003
the story that is me!
and you!

TIME MEASURED OUT!

I didn't want you to die!
   I wanted to clasp your neck
      and beg you to snuggle close,
         to protect me and
            hold me tight

But you died,
   and I have no one
      to protect me
      today—
         but me.

THE SOUND OF HER VOICE

August 24, 2002

The sound of her voice
   Saying my name,
Reverberates back to
   The very first time.

The time she held me in her arms
   For that first time
   And said my name.

No fruit tastes sweeter,
   No bell rings clearer.
Nothing soothes my soul
   Like hearing my mother saying,
      "Larada."

Chapter Five

2002

This set of poems spans a range of topics, spiced up with a lot of magical realism. During a Natalie Goldberg workshop, I jumped into magical realism, which I was introduced to in my Spanish literature classes back in the late 1980s. Just like it says —magical realism adds some magic to something real and shows things from a different perspective.

Teaching has its ups and downs. I turn to poetry to share this movement of my teacher career.

And finally, Ted and I marry—after all the struggles!

MEET LARADA

2002
Natalie Goldberg Workshop

I am turquoise, red, hot pink
And purple, a kaleidoscope
Of color rearranging
Changing as the parts of
Me fall into place.

The turquoise reflects the
Peace and calm deep within me
      Like the waters
         Of the Mexican Caribbean.

The red in me ignites into a flame—
Passionate and energetic
      But hot to touch.

The hot pink cries out
Notice me, I'm present—
You can't ignore me
  Anymore.

The purple states my power
That place inside me that has
Matured to womanhood
  But still holds a girlish twinkle.

A waltz,
A jitterbug, a swing dance,
The Latin rhythm of rumba,
  Or bolero.

The depth of me expresses itself
  In dance,
The spiritual connection to
  The music,
The beat,
The magic, and the sway!

The me totally revealed on
The dance floor,
Vulnerable,
Bare,
Connected to my partner
  And me
   And the song.

INTELLIGENCE TEST

2002
Natalie Goldberg Workshop

I catch shooting stars
    With my tongue.
Cold, icy trails of light
Pierce my tongue
    Deep
Reaching for the core of
    Ice in my heart.

Reaching to melt
One more layer,
But hopefully,
    It's the last!

The sparks from the shooting stars
Glaze the corner of my mouth,
Turning a frown

Into a smile.

Then the smile travels
All the way to my core
On the path of the stars,
    Like an electric shock.

Clearly, the touch of those
Shooting stars
Gently creased a wrinkle
In my soul,
    Wanting more of me
    Then I wanted to give.

    A star shines!
    A shooting star travels
    And my heart now knows
        The pierce of those stars.

    I don't want to know this much.
    Shooting stars, go home—
    Fly back through my being,
    Pierced my tongue,
    Leave me to solitude
        And aloneness.

    You started something
        I can't finish.

THE WOUNDED PRAYER

I loved teaching, and in my sixteen years, I faced many great experiences. After the occurrence of a life-threatening experience at a low-income school, I faced a different issue at a high-income school—parents upset with my strict classroom management. I became more strict because I was managing a computer lab and that required a watchful eye. Sadly, I faced criticism and censor for asking students to be responsible for their behavior.

February 5, 2002

Sixteen years of teaching
Each quiet dawn began
    With a blessing
    For each student,
        Whispered from my heart
            Music from my soul
            Lighting the day
                With clarity and peace

Day in
Day out
180 days a year plus weekends
And vacations.

Summer break came with relief and joy,
But
I started fresh for the next group,
The next year,
Positive energy
For a good vacation
And
A good start with me!

Solemnly I believed
It my duty,
Like grading papers,
Tests
And
Prayers!

No methods class taught me this.
No principal demanded it.
It wasn't circled on my yearly evacuation
Or a part of my professional
Development plan.

It came from
My spiritual nature,
My soul that longs for
The best for our next generation,
A gentle lullaby of background music
That played

TIME MEASURED OUT!

Throughout the day,
Started in that space
before the day begins.
A part of the mixture of
what drove me
to teach.
A part of my job as sure as anything.

❀

I used to pray for my students
Daily,
But not today.
Today I pray for
Protection from them.

In 1999
A gun brought to school to kill me,
Yet I wasn't there.
My substitute teacher dealt with it!
Even though I wasn't there,
Fear vibrated through me
And still does,
The sound of that bullet
That wasn't shot still rings
In my ears,
But I kept praying,
Harder and more diligently.

Last year,
Accused of humiliating students
Because I disciplined them,
Me in trouble,

Their behavior not questioned.
Me, the focus
The students absolved
      With no consequences.
The consequences were threats
      Against me
And my future at this school.

My focus lost!
   Worry set in
      With gut-wrenching anxiety,
      Every pass by my school mailbox
   Or
      Check of my school voice mail
   Or
      A lingering look
         From an administrator.

No longer
         Concentrating on lesson plans,
               Tests,
                     But
                           Still prayers.

Vigilantly I worried that I would err.
   Months passed.
      No problems.
      I thought I had figured it out.

BUT—

Last week,
   Accused of humiliating again,

My consequences more severe
    This time—
I asked students to be responsible
  For their behavior,
    The result—
  I got disciplined!
They participated in my consequences!
They signed affidavits
  And were empowered.
My power was taken!

It's all changed.
Today I see the classroom
  Through different eyes,
    Tainted!

I can't pray for them anymore,
  The desire is gone!
  The spirit is gone,
    The yearning to bless.

I want a mantel of protection,
  So I pray like I used to,
  But today, it is not for my students—
    It's for me!

I question every word I say
  Hypervigilant
  Observing myself as a teacher
  Criticizing and scrutinizing.

This wounded prayer hurts!

THE REWARD OF TEACHING

2002

One day after sixteen years of
Sixth grade classrooms, names, and faces,
Thousands of students
Discouragement,
And despair.
Faces fade into faces,
Names blend into one.

One day, at the airport
Going through security,
I saw a familiar face,
Older but familiar,
And he recognized me.

He called my name;
I called his.
We exchanged a hug
And shared the happenings of
8 to 9 years apart.

Miss Horner,
I have a great life,
My job,
My fiancé,
My future.
I have a great life.

I see clearly
Through his eyes
The rewards of teaching,
The joy!

I made a difference!

One student succeeded
Grew
Took what I taught
And grew up!

ADVENTURE ABOUNDS

March 12, 2002

Adventure abounds
But I don't want to be here.
My hands tied behind my back,
I'm forced into this dark, dark cave.

Right before I enter,
A yellow poppy brushes my cheek,
And I smell its sacred smell.

Acrid smells surround me
As I stepped down, deeper and deeper—

Hugging the wall to the left,
The only light I see is that
In front of me—
I keep swallowing my fears
As the dark surrounds me
More and more
Choking me
Taking my breath into fiery hands.

Pleasant this is not
Until my name is called
And the gentle poet-gardener
　　takes my hand.
A sob escapes through clenched teeth.
I had not realized my rigid stance.

Chichen Itza, Mexico - Taken by Larada Horner-Miller

"You're safe with me now," he consoles.
Gently, he leads me to the jungle
Surrounding Chichen Itza.
"Esta bien, mi hija.
Vamos conmigo a un lugar que tiene
Seguridad para ti."

Those glorious Spanish words melt my
Heart, and away we go.
His short Mayan stance comforts
    Me, and
Returns me to another time and place.

He's safe! We've done this before—
He cured my multitudes of
Mosquito bites.
He guided me to find my crystal.
He allowed me to fill my pockets
with pottery shards of the
Mayan and bring them home to enjoy!
He is Mayan to me.

He is safe!

A UNIQUE SCOOTER RIDE TO MARRIAGE

April 14, 2002

"Shall we do it?"
"Yes," I replied.

A unique scooter ride
For the pending bride.

I wore a turquoise T-shirt and capris.
He wore armor of steel.

We did the official requirements,
Paid the bucks,
Then rode the scooter to the chapel.

Again the official,
Then the minister stood in front of us
In the waiting room.

And she asked Ted the question.
He said, "I do!"
That stunned me!

She asked me, and I responded.
He kissed his bride,
    And it was done.

He said, "Let's celebrate!"

We danced the weekend away.

You said nothing would be different,
    But it is!
You made a vow, a legal agreement
    To do all that stuff—
And it shocked me!

FAUNCHING AT THE BIT

April 14, 2002

The silent echoes through my soul
As I stand on land that's mine,
And was my dad's
And granddad's.

Their spirits speak through the silence,
    Loud and strong!
The wind kisses my cheek
    As they pass by.
A meadowlark's twill continues.
    The spirit talk.

And whose voices before theirs?
Native, Hispanic, Frenchmen's
    Touched the earth,
        Where I now stand.

Our footprints commingle, and
    We become one,
Not separated by time or space.

A large spacious place opens up
    Inside me,
        And they walk through me—
All of them—
And I'm taken back to my roots
    To face humanity.

.

Chapter Six

2003 – CONNIE'S THIRTIETH BIRTHDAY POEMS

My niece, Connie, turned thirty, and our family showered her with love in a variety of ways. Her mother created a wonderful scrapbook with contributions from different family members. I wrote poetry for her and included pictures as my contribution. At this point, her life had many ups and downs.

A CIRCLE CAN'T BE BROKEN

February 14, 2003

A circle can't be broken.
    By its very nature,
The strength and continuity keep it
    together.

This circle of love will never be broken.

The years rolled by quickly—
    yesterday you were born
    today you are 30, a parent yourself.

It seems like yesterday
    We sat and giggled,
    enjoyed the splendor
        of this shared meal.

Hearts break
   Life happens

We've all grown older,
   but the people that are
      linked in this picture
         are connected forever!

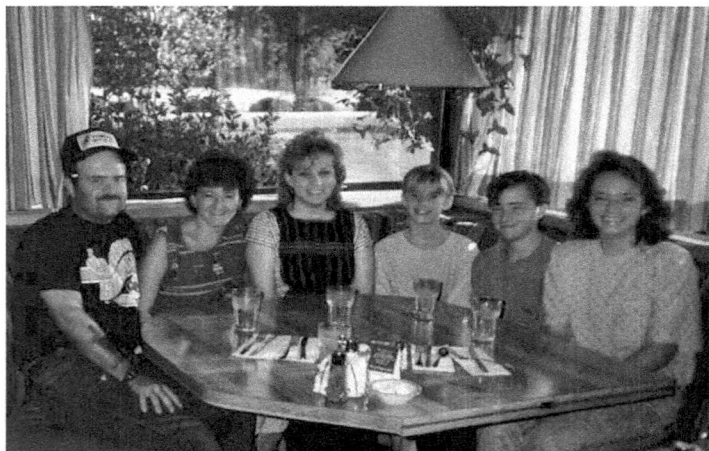

My brother's family and me

We love each other,
   share hurts
   share sorrow
   share joys!

We will continue!

CONNIE, HOLD ON

February 14, 2003

Connie, hold on—
 hold on to the people that love you
  have loved you forever

Hold on tight
 life batters and bruises
 your pain is mine
 mine is yours

Hold on tight
  we share blood
  Granddad's courses through your veins
    and raises its dusty,
     manured-covered head every once
      in a while—
        do you recognize it?
    Grannie's runs there also,
     purple and rich
      with you and me.
    We share the same—
     blood, last name, hurt, and joys.

Hold on tight,
  because I will be there
  we will be there
  forever.

SPRING BREAK BABY

February 14, 2003

Spring break hit on your due date
    so Mom and I drove to Kansas!
        to an event,
        to a happening,
        by God's design—to your birth!

To the eighteen-year-old girl that I was,
    your birth was spectacular
    and smacked of promises of the birth
    or births I would experience
        in the years to come.

As it turned out,
    yours is the only birth I shared—
    the night before
        you kicked and punched
        inside your mom,
            ready to come to us.

We were there—
    Grannie, Mamma, and me.
We laughed; you kicked.
My trembling hand dared to feel
    that life preparing to come out.

A restless night
    your dad went to work
    your mom uncomfortable—

then off to the hospital.

The Army accepted
    grandmothers,
    but not aunts.
I stayed anyway.
I fought to see you.
We waited
    the hours drug on.

Your dad ran down the hall shouting,
    "It's a Connie! It's a Connie!"
Within thirty minutes,
    I fought that old Army nurse
        to see you,
            and the miracle was complete.

TIME MEASURED OUT!

You looked at me, directly in the eye—
    the most beautiful baby
      in the world!

Yours is the only birth I've shared
    The world went on.

I married, divorced, remarried,
    and divorced.
      No children

Now thirty years later,
    a childless woman
      of almost fifty years today,
    you are thirty.

Yours is the only birth I've shared.
    I didn't carry you
      or feel the birth pangs—
    I've never had that privilege,
    but thirty years ago,
      your mom and dad shared your day
        with me—
      and you are mine,
        in a very special way.

I HOLD PRECIOUS THINGS TIGHT!

February 14, 2003

I hold precious things tight in my hand
    afraid to let them go,
    wanting that moment to last forever.

If only I hold on,
    it will stay the same;
    I can keep it
        capture it
            suffocate it!

I hold you tightly
    in pictures,
    favorite pictures of you
        a baby, newborn, wide-eyed,
            looking me straight in the eye
            and saying with those eyes,
                "I know you."

a toddler dressed up in
a bikini,
a bright paper sombrero
from Casa Bonita,
and slick plastic clogs,
laced with your giggles
and mine.
the circle of us—a smiling group
enjoying the time we had together
Graduation—you so beautiful,
eighteen and grown up,
and I wept.

I hold you tightly in my heart,
but I don't want you to suffocate.
Can I stop it?

My pain started when young—
inflicted on me—
Was your pain inflicted on you?
Do you realize your pain today?
Does it have a name?
a face?
Mine does!

I hold you close to my heart,
but my fingers uncurl,
let go,
relax,
rejoice!

Celebrate you!

Chapter Seven

2003 – RETURN TO SKETCHBOOK

I end this book with a return to my sketchbook, with topics ranging from nature to the war in Iraq and wondering about peace. Is it possible?

I end with a poem dedicated to my mom.

SAFETY IN NATURE'S CHURCH

January 5, 2003
Mesa, Arizona

This morning, driving through the saguaros outside of Mesa, Arizona, I had a spiritual experience. The gentle giants with their arms raised to the heavens provided a rich Sunday morning ritual of praise and gratitude. The morning sunshine filtered through lacy high clouds, giving an ethereal glow to the day and the earth.

The saguaros' spires were lifted up in union but disjointed, uneven, sporadic. The horizon's line of shapely saguaros appeared whiskered, a beard of not stubble, but good healthy growth of saguaros.

Mostly singular solitary creatures, but joined in community here, there, and everywhere.

Character and difference defined each saguaro—no two alike yet all with one mission—arm or arms raised to the heavens in praise and gratitude—deeply rooted in the pungent barren desert earth. Solid and strong.

Nature's Church

It was nature's church
  A soft Sunday morning ritual
  I stumbled onto—an intruder,
    an outsider
  But very welcome.

It was nature's worshipers
  Saguaros with arms raised high
    In praise and gratitude,
    A hallelujah chorus
    Silent yet loud!

Worshippers of the great Creator!
  No fighting over doctrine or sect
    No judgment or hatred!
Sheer unadulterated worship,
  Joy, praise
Gathered on a Sunday morning
Physically distant
  Spaced on the countryside,
  But spiritually united
  With me
    In one mission!
Rooted deeply in the barren desert earth!

My spirit stood up
 Near one particularly distinct saguaro
 And I copied the raised arms
 And let my spirit join in with
 The heavenly chorus
  on that Arizona hillside!

THE QUIET WISE POET-GARDENER

January 22, 2003

My spirit didn't die the
    day you tried to crush me.

Instead I went deep inside and
    became quiet and wise.

You tried to take my words away,
    instead the poet took those words and
        grew them deep inside.
            A fragile life was formed.

I grew;
    words sheltered
        and hid in my soul,
            waited to be born.

THE QUIET WISE POET-GARDENER

The poet-gardener watered that spirit
  and those words,
      A dark space in my soul,
        an incubation of new life.

Years of life and pain and hurt passed,
  and words grew quietly and wise
    deep inside.

I knew they were there
  because they comforted me often,
    a soothing lullaby sometimes.

At other times, words escaped,
  washing over my being
    demanding to be said,
      so I did.

Green, ripe, full, mature
  and blossomed,
    a vine ripened tomato
      ready for the pickin'.

This poet-gardener co-created
  this wonder, allowing me
    to have a voice
                and my words.

WAR—PRIME TIME!

March 26, 2003

War—Prime Time!
Is war ever the answer?
Can a fight bring peace?

CNN measures out the war in Iraq
      In bits and pieces—
            Live coverage
            Better coverage
            Up-to-date coverage
But what if I don't want to know?
      At least a part of me!

Part of me wants to watch
      To catch sight of the blood
            And the gore,
                  To know the facts,
                  To see it firsthand.

It's insatiable
   Addictive!

But part of me is injured by every word,
         By every photo,
         By every explosion,
And feels shell-shocked already!
   After only five days!

Prime Time war—
   Reality TV at its worst!
     Real casualties
       Real pain
         Real destruction
And it sells a lot of hamburgers
   and cars!

PEACE—ELUSIVE PEACE

March 26, 2003

Peace
    Elusive peace

A fresh snowfall
    The laughter of a child
        A deep breath and
         centeredness from meditation

I seek peace
    But cause war.
I seek peace
    But am an amateur
        Because all I feel is anguish!
I seek peace.
    But wonder
        if it's really possible for long.
The "buts" kill me!

God is peace!
    Peace is possible in this moment
        Only!
    Joy is possible now!

Pain covers me like a dark shroud
    Breathing its death dirge into my ear,
    Wanting to kill me.
    Proclaiming suicide the answer.

My vision is impaired!
    I see only doom and destruction.

Pain becomes my every breath!

Can I seek peace when consumed
    by pain?
        Can I ever recognize it?

Pain becomes my life;
    Peace, the illusion!

The lie grows, and peace is only
    possible in the afterlife
        Or for the chosen few
        Or not at all!

Do I believe the lie?

Who told me the lie
    with such convincing strength?
Where did it originate?

THE SOUND OF THE TRAIN

September 23, 2003

The sound of a train
　　The shrill whistle
　　The rumbling of wheels on tracks
Echoed through my childhood,
　　To one precious moment.

Our sleepy little country town
　　Edged by the train.

　　A train ride from our small
Town in southeastern Colorado—
　　20 miles to Folsom, New Mexico
A legitimate field trip for
　　First graders.

THE SOUND OF THE TRAIN

When I left town in that train,
   I never looked back.
   My future was set—
Traveling became the love of my life!

MY HEART WAS TOUCHED!

September 30, 2003

Can something, someone outside of you
Reach deep inside your heart
And touch it?
Mine has been!
At various times, for variety
Of reasons.

I loved his touch
Soft and scratchy at the same time
One eye blue, one brown
That looked deep into my soul
Hot sticky breath
That smelled of bones and dirt
A dry crusty nose that sniffed the air
And smelled me
And shouted his delight
By running in circles

A tail that wagged his whole body
  In exuberance for life
A coat of fur—black, white, brown,
  And gold—
    A luscious mixture of color.

Patches, my dear dog!

Patches died April 16, 2003.
  His animal instinct drove him
    Into the back of our yard
      To die alone.
  But we carried him
    Into our living room,
      Where he died between us

I stayed up—
  While death methodically took him
    Away.
  He labored for breath.
He stirred from his struggle,
  Lifted his head,

Drank a sip of water
    But dropped to the floor again.

I went to bed
    Him barely holding on,
    My heart breaking.
I slept fitfully
    And woke to the sure knowledge
      He was dead.

I touched his lifeless form,
But the vitality that was Patches
    Was gone.
His fur still felt soft and scratchy,
    But the life that pulsated through him
      Was gone,
And the touch was so different,
    So foreign.

It was his life,
    His joy,
    His delight with being our dog
      I could feel
      When I touched his splendid coat,
      When his eyes touched me
        With his vigor.

And now it was gone,
    And I sobbed!

HERE'S YOUR LIFE, ELVA MARIE DICKERSON HORNER

Mom and I celebrated her seventy-fifth birthday in California with my brother's family. I wrote this poem and my nieces and nephew read it like a Poem-in-Three Voices at her party.

Here's Your Life, Elva Marie Dickerson Horner

Summer, 2003

February 13, 1919, a young couple rode
    horseback
        to marry
            Virgil & Tresia
Nine months later, Willa Lee came
Nine years later, Elva Marie was born
    on September 24, 1928.

Your story starts here!

Youngest child,
Dirt floors in your home,
Ma and Pa close
Violin lessons
Donald Lujan called you "Squeaky."

A move to Raton when you were
    in the eighth grade.
In high school you hung out with
    the country kids
        from Johnson Mesa.
You went to see the play *Othello*
    and were mystified.
Hughie and Willie were married
    and along came Janet.
        You played with her like a doll.

And you loved to dance.
    A certain cowboy caught your eye
        at a dance.
You noticed his different dance style.

At the Robin Hood
    in Raton, New Mexico,
He crossed the dance floor
    toward you.
You knew he was going to ask you
    to dance,
        you panicked.
And the romance of a lifetime started
    with Harold Horner.

You dated:
  you danced!
You got thrown out of the Crystal
    Lounge
  because you were underage,
But he returned
  when you turned twenty-one.

You were married on August 28, 1951
  in Raton, New Mexico.
Your married life that would span
  forty-five years had begun.
You immediately became stepmother
  to three small children:
      Fred, Larraine, and Sue.

As newlyweds you moved in with
    your in-laws in Branson, Colorado
      to experience a small-town
          tradition—Chevarier
    Short sheet the beds,
    Remove labels off of all
      the canned goods,
    A wheelbarrow ride for the bride

Your first home was bought from
    the Stevensons—
        Lock, stock, and barrel.

On May 25, 1952,
    Harold Virgil arrived;
On June 27, 1953,
    Teresa Larada appeared
— 13 months later!

Your family intact!

Lots of life happened in that small
    country town through the years.
The children grew—
    Dad remembers coming home
        From La Junta and caught you
        In the rocking chair
        With the baby in each arm.
Your arms were numb!

You painted bright red lips
    for the thin-lipped Larada.
You spanked us with a wooden spoon.
You shampooed our hair
    And sculpted it to stand up
        Straight and tall.

Bub caught his hand
    In the washing machine wringer—
You ran next door to Edna Fry
    For help.

School filled the fall and winter
    With basketball, dances, and
        Cheerleading.
Spring was calving, baseball,
    And branding.
Summer was Little League, horses,
    4H, and our county fair,
Our one family vacation every year.

And lots of children at our house
    Because you made them feel
        So welcome!

Marriages—Lela joined our family!

Nine grandchildren came
    Connie, Andy, Cheryl,
    Jeff, Wade, Ellen,
    Jason, Travis, and Blake

Eleven great grandchildren,
    and one on the way.

You cherish family, get-togethers,
    And holidays.
Granddad Horner loved to have family
Get-togethers at our house because of
    Your cooking and hospitality!

After Granddad Horner died,
    You became dad's right-hand man,
    Able to do anything on the ranch—
    You worked hard!

You and Dad enjoyed a remarkable
   Relationship of shared interest:
      You danced, traveled,
        Work together, and loved people.

You lovingly cared for Dad
   To the end—
And you have taken care of yourself
   These last few years admirably

Your interests vary.

You're an avid sports fan
   Of all the Branson sports;
You yelled loudly at basketball games
   With Mary Arguello.
You now sit in the same place every game
   With Doris Goff.

You have been involved in the Branson
   Home Demonstration Club,
Now Craft Club
   And Community Club
Working in PTA for many years,
   You helped start the annual
      junior high basketball tournament.

In the 70s,
   You got interested in genealogy
      And have researched both
        The Dickerson and
          Horner sides extensively.

Girlfriends have been a part of
　　Your life forever—
　　　　Ellin Berry in high school;
　　　　Clara Warner, Nancy Salas,
　　　　and Mokey McMillan
　　　　　　Years ago;
　　　　Helen Waldroup, Betty Clark,
　　　　　　And Rose Ward now.

You were baptized
　　And are a faithful member of
　　　　Des Moines Methodist Church,
　　Attending every Sunday
　　　　With Bill & Janet.

All of us have evidence
　　Of your beautiful handiwork:
　　　　Afghans, quilts,
　　　　　　Christmas ornaments,
　　　　　　　　And so much more.

In 1999, we took a trip
　　To Eastern Europe
　　To find information
　　　　about your great grandfather—
　　　　　　It was a trip of a lifetime.

Often when we are with you,
　　We get the privilege of
　　　　Hearing your laughter,
　　　　　　So rich and inviting
　　　　Seeing your eyes twinkle.

Here are some memories
   That make your blue eyes sparkle:
The first time Harold Horner asked
   You to dance
Connie making milkshakes with you
   And it ended up on the floor
Andy looking through the Remington
   Cowboy book together with you
     And making up stories
Cheryl drawing the
     "God don't make Junk" picture
       for you
   And you sitting the whole time
   watching
    her draw.
   You still have it on your refrigerator.
The twins loved going to the trailer
   And playing baseball with you.

Mom, what a wonderful life
   We celebrate today —
     75 glorious years!

Elva Marie Horner at her 75th birthday party in California

HIS EYES

Christmas 2003

I turned 50—
   My tastes have changed
      over the years.

Before tight Wrangler jeans
   And a cute butt caught my eye.
A specific man was what I wanted
   Looks, physique—
      Definite requirements.

Years changed me—

He races across my heart
   Like a wild colt running free,
      Mane and tail flying
         in the breeze.

HIS EYES

What is it in him that grabs me?
    The cute butt, the brute build
        No longer top my list.
    His butt most definitely is cute,
      But it is . . .

His eyes
    Sapphire blue
        That captivate me
           With a sparkle,
                A joyful reflection of me.
        Burn with desire
        Laugh without words
        Communicate quickly
Blue boyish eyes that want to play
    and need a playmate.

I lose myself in the smell
    Of that one secret place.

The smell of his neck
    My favorite place to snuggle close
        To him
    And lap up the smell that's
        So familiar.
           What is it?

His smell
    In that one particular spot
        The mixture
           Of leather and sweat
           Nuts and bolts
               His life sweated out.

THE FRAGRANT LILAC OF MY LIFE!

Christmas, 2003

She is Mom,
but she is more!

A knot chokes in my throat as
I look at her profile, so familiar—
an outline of her nose and chin
etched in my memory.
She's the fragrant lilac of my life!

Seventy-five years she celebrated
this year!

I watch her walk
   cautious, after cataract surgery
   brushing a toe, a foot forward
     gingerly
       and awkward
Her life changing before me.

I sit next to her
   and laugh
     Two little girls enjoying
      each other,
        not mother and daughter

Her teasing causes
   a giggle so deep
   it rumbles in my
   belly and my childhood.

She has often made me laugh
   a playmate that stirs
   a ridiculous side of me,
My first playmate.

We wrestle,
   the laughter goes deeper.
The joy I feel in our
   physical contact rings
   heavenly.

Here this close to me—
I smell her sweet scent,
   a mixture of life,
   love and pain and sweat.

Our laughter continues
    and I smile deeply
    My heart smiles
    in remembrance.

This is the woman
    who carried me close
    to her heart,
    and we still live there
    when we laugh.

CONCLUSION

In the week of February 17-21, 2025, Fr. Richard Rohr shared his metaphor, The Cosmic Egg, in his daily meditation I receive in my inbox, and his explanation struck me. I immediately saw a connection in my writing. He sees the world as having four story structures: *My Story, Our Story, Others Stories,* and *The Story*.

In all my books, I share *My Story,* whether in poetry or prose, memoir or historical fiction. A small-town Colorado girl's life became unexpectedly rich. Often, I share vulnerable parts of my life. It spills over in my words.

That said, I tell *Our Story*, a rich mosaic of being a country girl, a beautician, a middle school teacher, a square and round dancer, a world traveler, a knitter, and a cat lover. A divorcee. In my seventies now. A Baby Boomer. I lived through the 60s and 70s, the Beatles, and Meryl Haggard. The Vietnam War and the draft. I'm in recovery, and it has shaped my life in so many ways. After my parents died, my brother and I were left our family ranch, which we co-own and co-manage.

Many of you identify with one or more of those pieces of

my life—that's where *Our Story* intersects, and that's probably the reason you're reading this book. Something in the description, the cover art, or the poems touched your heart and you said, "Yes, I feel that way!"

The *Others Stories* may also compel you to read my work, because you see me as someone so totally different and opposite from you. You brave the world of our differences and desire a view into my world. Somehow you felt something I had to say might add to your worldview.

And last, *The Story*, the overarching story that we all share, holds many truths that we all embrace: love, anger, forgiveness, joy, sadness, and happiness. I hope this book contains many.

I wrestled with many major issues in my forties, as some of you may have, and with the help of poetry, I came out on the other side—resilient!

For me, any life event generates a poem. From the quiet shores of Alaska to the trembling aftermath of September 11th, these poems chart not just my path but our collective one. They hold grief for my father, the complexities of breaking up with my ex-husband and getting back together again, finally marrying, and the shifting perspective that comes with teaching young minds as the world transforms around us. So much was packed into four short years, but my eyes stayed wide open to see what this world had to offer.

Without even knowing it, I've followed Mary Oliver's instructions for living a life:

> "Pay attention.
> Be astonished.
> Tell about it."[1]

---

1. 1. Mary Oliver, *Devotions*, (Penguin Press, 2017), 105.

And the journey continues beyond these pages. I hope that throughout this book you've found moments that resonated with your own journey through this unpredictable life. Poetry isn't about perfect rhymes or distant metaphors—it's about witnessing the world with eyes wide open, capturing the extraordinary within ordinary days.

If you've ever thought about writing poetry, I hope this encourages you to do it. Don't be fearful or reluctant. Celebrate life—not only the wins, but the struggles too. Pay attention and be astonished, like Mary Oliver says.

You never know what amazing things your journey can bring you.

ABOUT THE AUTHOR

Award-winning author Larada Horner-Miller weaves rich stories across multiple genres, from heartfelt memoirs to insightful poetry. With numerous literary accolades to her name, including Book Excellence Awards recognition, she seamlessly moves between historical biographies, personal reflections, and lyrical verse. Her diverse catalog reflects both scholarly precision and emotional authenticity, drawing from her background in education and deep connections to her southwestern roots.

She has written eight award-winning books and three cookbooks. She has also recorded three audiobooks.

Larada now lives with her husband in Boquete, a town in western Panama.

Grab a free poetry chapbook featuring Larada's poetry from two poetry classes she took in 2002 and 2003 to sample more of her poetry here: https://laradasfreebook.com/truth

Interested in more information about Larada:
www.laradasbooks.com
larada@laradasbooks.com

ALSO BY LARADA HORNER-MILLER

Explore all nine of Larada Horner-Miller's acclaimed books, listed below in publication order. This multi-award-winning author moves effortlessly between memoir, poetry, and biography, bringing scholarly insight and emotional truth to every page. Each book stands alone as a powerful read—together, they showcase a literary career worth celebrating. Start anywhere, read everywhere.

- **This Tumbleweed Landed: Life in the 50s & 60s in Rural America**
- **When Will Papa Get Home?**
- **Let Me Tell You a Story**
- **A Time to Grow Up: A Daughter's Grief Memoir**
- **Just Another Square Dance Caller: Authorized Biography of Marshall Flippo**
- **Coronavirus Reflections: Bitter or Better?**
- **Hair on Fire: A Heartwarming & Humorous Christmas Memoir**

- **Is My Truth Universal: A Woman's Poetic Journey - FREE POETRY CHAPBOOK**
- **Was It a Dream?: Navigating Life's Journey Through Poetry**

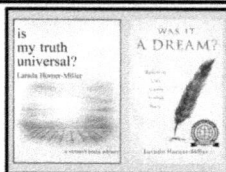

FUTURE PROJECTS

- *An Eye Witness to Life* —Auto-fiction: Part fiction, part autobiography
- A five-book poetry book series continues after Book 1 - *Was It a Dream?: Navigating Life's Journey Through Poetry,* Book #2 - *Time Measured Out!: Navigating Life's Journey Through Poetry*
- A haiku poetry book
- How to write a biography—based on what I learned in writing the Marshall Flippo biography
- And one more Tumbleweed book—more poems & stories about growing up in the Branson, Colorado area! There are so many!

AND NOW, WOULD YOU. . .?

I love this book because it continues my poetry life. Each poem amazes me with its imagery and details.

Reviews, reviews, reviews—they help the sale of books. If you liked this book, please go to laradasbooks.com to find links to the book and write a review and rate—that would really help me.

EXCERPT FROM BOOK #3 OF NAVIGATING LIFE'S JOURNEY THROUGH POETRY SERIES

Familiarity

March 23, 2004
Spring Break

The moon kissed my lips
    And the most sensual kiss
    I've ever known.

Deep yearning burned in me.

Seduced by nature's light,
    The kiss pierced my soul,
    Jolting me into an altered state.

Could we make love?
    Could my desire be fulfilled?

I pound on the door of familiarity,
    And say, "stop – open!
      I must pass through! "
Chained to the familiar,
    I brace myself to break through!

But the familiar holds me shackled
    To the old
    To the pain
    To the unhealed

www.ingramcontent.com/pod-product-compliance
Lightning Source LLC
Chambersburg PA
CBHW072345090426
42741CB00012B/2923